UNLEASH YOUR BUSINESS POTENTIAL

The **Expert Guide** to **Planning** a **Loan** for **Sustainable Growth** and **Financial Freedom**

UNLEASH YOUR BUSINESS POTENTIAL

The **Expert Guide** to **Planning** a **Loan** for **Sustainable Growth** and **Financial Freedom**

MUKESH PANDEY

Worldwide Published by
Pendown Press

PENDOWN PRESS LLP
An ISO 9001 & ISO 14001 Certified Co.
Regd. Office 3767A, Kanhaiya Nagar,
Tri Nagar, Delhi-110035
Ph.: 8130886000, 9650072927, 8595249536
E-mail: info@pendownpress.com
Branch Office 1A/2A, 20, Hari Sadan, Ansari Road,
Daryaganj, New Delhi-110002
Ph.: 011-45794768
Website: PendownPress.com

First Edition: 2023
Price: ₹ 299/-
ISBN: 978-93-5554-782-8

Layout and Cover Designed by Pendown Graphics Team
Printed and Bound in India by Thomson ress India Ltd.

Dedication

To all the ambitious entrepreneurs and avid business enthusiasts,

This book is dedicated to those who dare to dream, to those who envision a future where their businesses flourish and financial freedom becomes a reality. It's for the go-getters who are ready to take their ventures to new heights, and make informed decisions that lead to sustainable growth.

We're inspired by your dedication to creating something meaningful, your determination to learn from your mistakes and your commitment to achieving financial stability inspires us. We wrote this book with you in mind — because we believe that understanding the nuances of borrowing and loans is a crucial step on your journey to success.

May this book serve as a guiding light, illuminating your path to financial prosperity. Let it furnish you with the knowledge and tools needed to make wise financial decisions, avoid pitfalls, and ultimately pave the way for your business's sustainable growth and your own financial freedom.

Within these pages, we unravel the complexities of borrowing in a way that's straightforward and easy to grasp. We dive deep into the seven most common mistakes entrepreneurs often commit when seeking loans for their businesses. Our goal is to empower you with knowledge, to arm you with insights, and to equip you with the tools needed to navigate the world of financing.

Always remember, mistakes serve as valuable lessons for growth and improvement. By recognizing and addressing these common missteps, you'll be better prepared to unlock the full potential of your business. With the right guidance and a commitment to smart financial decisions, you can chart a course towards sustainable growth and the financial freedom you've always envisioned.

Here's to your journey of unlocking business potential, making impactful choices, and securing a prosperous future.

With heartfelt appreciation,

Mukesh Pandey

Contents

> "Money is only a tool. It will take you wherever you wish,
> but it will not replace you as the driver."
>
> ~Ayn Rand

Preface

Welcome to "Unleash Your Business Potential for Sustainable Growth and Financial Freedom." In this book, we are embarking on a journey to explore the fundamental principles that have the power to propel your business towards success, all while shedding light on the often-overlooked pitfalls that can hinder your progress. Our focus? Loans—the double-edged sword that can either fuel your aspirations or shackle your dreams.

In the modern business landscape, loans have become an integral tool for expansion, innovation, and capitalization. Yet, they also come with inherent risks that, if not managed wisely, can result in severe repercussions. As entrepreneurs and business owners, it's crucial to equip ourselves with the knowledge and insights to make informed decisions when it comes to borrowing funds.

In the pages that follow, we will delve into the heart of the matter—identifying and dissecting the seven common mistakes that many of us make when considering, applying for, and managing loans. Drawing from real-world examples, practical anecdotes, and expert perspectives, we aim to demystify the intricacies of business borrowing.

Our goal is simple: to empower you with the tools and awareness needed to navigate the complex world of business loans. Regardless of whether you're a startup founder seeking that crucial initial capital, a small business owner aiming to expand operations, or an established entrepreneur looking to fund a new venture, the insights within these chapters are tailored to help you make the best choices for your unique circumstances.

We will cover a spectrum of topics, including:

1. **Misaligned Goals:** Shedding light on the importance of aligning loan purposes with business objectives, ensuring that borrowed funds contribute to growth rather than short-term fixes.

2. **Over borrowing:** Mastering the art of borrowing the right amount—neither too little that hampers growth nor too much that creates a burden.

3. **Ignored Interest Rates:** Exploring the significance of interest rates and their various forms, enabling you to decipher the true cost of borrowing.

4. **Neglected Terms and Conditions:** Exploring the fine print to avoid unexpected surprises, while also mastering negotiation strategies.

5. **Lack of Repayment Strategy:** Crafting a well-defined plan to ensure timely loan repayment, fostering a healthy credit history and rapport with lenders.

6. **Ignoring Alternative Options:** Exploring alternative funding avenues beyond traditional loans, such as equity financing and grants.

7. **Blindness to Financial Health:** Emphasizing the need to evaluate your business's financial health before borrowing, safeguarding against unforeseen challenges.

By the time you've turned the last page, our aim is for you to possess a clear roadmap for navigating the world of business loans. Armed with this knowledge, you can confidently leverage loans as a stepping stone towards achieving your business goals, ensuring sustainability, and ultimately achieving the financial freedom you've always aspired to.

Remember, the journey to success is not about avoiding risks entirely, but about understanding and managing them wisely. We're excited to embark on this educational journey with you. Let's unlock your business potential, together.

Sincerely,

Mukesh Pandey

MD-Rupyaapaisa.com

Working Capital strategist and loan and mortgage expert

Introduction

Welcome to "Unleash Your Business Potential for Sustainable Growth and Financial Freedom." We're thrilled to have you embark on this journey with us as we explore the critical topic of loans and unveil the common mistakes that often go unnoticed. Whether you're a seasoned entrepreneur or just starting out on your business adventure, understanding how to navigate loans wisely is key to achieving your dreams.

In the upcoming pages, we'll be your guides as we dissect the world of loans and unveil the seven common mistakes that many of us unknowingly make when seeking financial support for our ventures. These mistakes can have significant consequences, impacting not only your business's growth but also your financial freedom.

Our goal is simple: to empower you with the knowledge you need to make well-informed decisions regarding loans. We want you to be equipped with the tools to avoid these pitfalls, enabling you to secure the funds you need while setting your business on a path toward long-term success.

We've all heard the saying, "Knowledge is power." In the realm of business and finance, this adage holds an exceptional significance. By the time you reach the end of this book, you'll have a clear understanding of the mistakes to watch out for and the strategies to employ for smarter loan decisions. We'll provide you with straightforward explanations and practical advice, ensuring that you're well-prepared to take your business to new heights.

So, whether you're considering a loan for expansion, acquire equipment, or bolster working capital, you're in the right place. Together, we'll delve into the intricacies of loans and financial choices, all with the aim of helping you unlock your business's potential for sustainable growth and, ultimately, achieve the financial freedom you've been working toward.

Let's dive in and uncover the secrets to smarter borrowing and better business outcomes. Your journey to success starts here.

Best regards,

Mukesh Pandey

Acknowledgements

Writing a book is a journey that requires the support, encouragement, and inspiration of numerous individuals. As I reflect on the creation of "Unleash Your Business Potential for Sustainable Growth and Financial Freedom," I am humbled by the many people who have played a pivotal role in bringing this work to fruition.

Commencing this book without acknowledging the people who have been part of this endeavor, and without whose support I wouldn't have reached where I am today, would leave a significant gap. It gives me immense pleasure to express my gratitude to everyone who dedicated their valuable time and efforts to collaborate with me.

First and foremost, my eternal gratitude goes to my Guruji; Shri Ashustosh Maharaj ji. I would like to express my heartfelt gratitude to my mentor, Mr. Akshar Yadav, and the entire Get Overbooked family. Your unwavering dedication to personal and professional growth has been a constant source of motivation for me. Your passion for learning, innovation, and pushing the boundaries of what's possible has inspired me to delve deeply into the subject matter of this book. Without your influence, this project may never have come to be.

I also want to extend my sincere thanks to the individuals who contributed their expertise, insights, and feedback throughout the writing process. Your valuable input has enriched the content and ensured its accuracy and relevance. Your commitment to excellence shines through in every chapter, and I am truly grateful for your contributions.

To my dear family and friends, thank you for your patience, understanding, and unwavering belief in me. Your encouragement during the highs and support during the lows have been instrumental in bringing this project to fruition. Your love and constant presence provide the foundation upon which I build my aspirations.

I also wish to extend my appreciation to the readers who will engage with this book. Your thirst for knowledge and commitment to growth are the reasons I embarked on this writing journey. It is my hope that the insights shared within these pages will empower you to make well-informed decisions and adeptly navigate the intricate landscape of business financing.

In closing, I am reminded that the creation of a book is a collaborative effort that extends beyond the boundaries of its pages. To everyone who has contributed, supported, and believed in this endeavor, I extend my deepest gratitude. May this book serve as a beacon of knowledge and inspiration for those who seek to unlock their business potential, achieve sustainable growth, and realize the financial freedom they rightfully deserve.

With heartfelt appreciation,

Mukesh Pandey

Chapter 1

Understanding the Different Types of Loans

Taking out a loan is a common financial decision that people make to fulfill various financial needs. When it comes to borrowing money, there are many different types of loans to choose from. Whether you're looking to fund a new business venture, purchase a car, or consolidate debt, understanding the different types of loans available to you can help you make an informed decision. In this chapter, we'll explore some of the most common types of loans and what makes each one unique.

Loans Against Property (LAP)

A loan against property, also known as a mortgage loan, is a secured loan backed by the borrower's property. These loans are commonly utilized to finance substantial expenses like education or home renovation projects. The **borrowing limit is determined by the property's value** and the borrower's creditworthiness. As these loans are secured, they generally offer lower interest rates compared to unsecured loans. However, the borrower faces the risk of losing their property in the event of loan default.

Unsecured Business Loans

Unsecured business loans are loans that are not backed by collateral. These loans are typically used to finance small business expenses such as inventory, equipment, and payroll. The **borrowing capacity of such loans** is typically based on the borrower's creditworthiness and business revenue. These loans typically have higher interest rates than secured loans due to the lack of collateral. **Nevertheless,** they can be a favorable choice for businesses lacking assets to offer as collateral.

Working Capital Loans

Working capital loans are short-term loans **options designed to support a** business's operational expenses. These loans are typically used to cover **essential** costs such as payroll, rent, and inventory. The **borrowing capacity of such loans** is **usually determined by** the business's revenue and creditworthiness. These loans can be either secured or unsecured. They typically have higher interest rates than longer-term loans, but they can be a good option for businesses that need to access cash quickly.

Home Loans

Home loans are a type of secured loan used for purchasing or constructing a home. These loans generally involve substantial amounts and have long repayment periods. The **borrowing capacity is determined by the property value** and the borrower's creditworthiness. As secured loans, they usually carry lower interest rates compared to unsecured loans. However, borrowers face the risk of losing their property in the event of loan default.

Machinery Loans

Machinery loans are a type of secured loan used for purchasing or upgrading machinery in a a business. These loans **generally involve substantial** amounts and have long repayment periods. The **borrowing capacity is determined by** the machinery's value and the borrower's creditworthiness. **As secured** loans, they typically carry lower interest rates compared to unsecured loans. However, borrowers face the risk of losing their machinery **in the event of loan default.**

Auto Loans

Auto loans are used to finance the purchase of a vehicle. These loans can be either secured or unsecured, and the borrowing amount is typically **determined by** the vehicle's and the borrower's creditworthiness. **In the case of a secured**

loan the lender has the right to repossess the vehicle if the borrower defaults. Auto loans generally have lower interest rates compared to unsecured loans.

Personal Loans

Personal loans are unsecured loans that can be used for various purposes, such as consolidating debt or financing a significant expense. The borrowing amount is typically based on the borrower's creditworthiness and income. These loans generally come with higher interest rates compared to secured loans, but they serve as a suitable option for borrowers without collateral to pledge.

In conclusion, gaining an understanding of the different types of loans available can assist you in making an informed decision when it comes to borrowing money. Before obtaining a loan, it's important to evaluate your financial situation and determine the loan type that best suits your needs. Whether you **intend** to fund a **substantial purchase or manage your debt, exploring the available options will help you make a well-informed choice.**

Understanding the Benefits and Risks of Taking out a Loan.

Borrowing money through a loan can be a useful tool for many people to finance large expenses or investments. However, it's important to carefully consider the benefits and risks before taking out a loan. In this chapter, we'll delve into the potential benefits and risks of borrowing through a loan in detail.

Benefits of Taking out a Loan

1. **Access to Capital** : One of the most significant benefits of taking out a loan is the access to capital that it provides. Loans allow individuals and businesses to obtain the funding necessary to make large purchases or investments that they would otherwise be unable to afford. This can be particularly useful in situations where cash flow is limited or when there is a need for immediate funding.

2. **Flexibility** : Loans can be structured in a variety of ways to meet the specific needs of borrowers. For example, borrowers can choose the length of the loan term, the interest rate, and the repayment schedule that works best for them. This flexibility allows borrowers to tailor the loan to their unique financial situation and budget.

3. **Credit Building** : Taking out a loan and making consistent, on-time payments can help improve a borrower's credit score. This can be particularly useful for individuals who have a limited credit history or are looking to improve their creditworthiness in order to qualify for future loans or credit lines.

4. **Tax Deductibility** : Certain types of loans, such as home equity loans or business loans, may qualify for tax deductions. This **potential tax benefit can effectively lower** the overall borrowing expenses and offer extra savings for borrowers.

Risks of Taking out a Loan

1. **Interest Costs** : The primary risk associated with taking out a loan is the cost of interest. Interest rates vary depending on the type of loan, the lender, and the borrower's creditworthiness. High interest rates can significantly increase the overall cost of the loan and make it more difficult to repay.

2. **Fees and Charges : Apart from** interest costs, borrowers may also face additional fees and charges when obtaining a loan. These charges encompass origination fees, prepayment penalties, and late payment fees. These charges can add up quickly and increase the overall cost of the loan.

3. **Risk of Default :** Taking out a loan also entails the risk of default. If a borrower becomes unable to make payments on the loan, they **face the possibility of damaging** their credit score and potentially **forfeiting** any collateral used to secure the loan. Defaulting on a loan may also lead to legal action initiated by the lender.

4. **Over borrowing :** Another risk of taking out a loan is overborrowing. Borrowers may **succumb** to **the temptation of** borrowing more than they truly need or can realistically repay, resulting in financial stress and challenges in meeting loan payments. Overborrowing can also **have adverse effects on** a borrower's credit score, making it harder to qualify for future loans.

Conclusion

Overall, taking out a loan can **offer substantial** benefits to borrowers, **such as** access to capital, flexibility, credit building, and potential tax deductibility. **Nevertheless,** borrowers must also **conscientiously assess** the risks associated with borrowing, encompassing interest costs, fees and charges, the risk of default, and the danger of overborrowing. **Prior to obtaining** a loan, it's important to carefully evaluate your financial situation, budget, and ability to repay the loan to ensure that it is a sound financial decision.

> "The lack of money is the root of all evil."
>
> ~Mark Twain

Chapter **2**

The Importance of Understanding the Terms and Conditions of a Loan

When taking out a loan, it's crucial to understand the terms and conditions of the loan agreement. Unfortunately, **numerous** borrowers fail to fully grasp the **intricacies** of their loan agreement, which can **result in** financial **difficulties in the future**. In this chapter, we'll explore the reasons why it's important to understand the terms and conditions of a loan and what borrowers can do to ensure they're making informed decisions.

The Risks of Not Understanding Loan Terms and Conditions

1. **Unexpected Fees and Charges:** One of the biggest risks of not understanding the terms and conditions of a loan is the possibility of unexpected fees and charges. Loan agreements can include various fees and charges, such as application fees, origination fees, prepayment penalties, and late payment fees.

If a borrower is not aware of these charges, they may find themselves facing unexpected costs that can make it difficult to repay the loan.

2. **Defaulting on the Loan** : Another risk of not understanding the terms and conditions of a loan is the **potential** for defaulting on the loan. Defaulting **transpires** when a borrower fails to make payments on the loan as agreed upon in the loan agreement. This can **lead to the imposition of** late fees, harm to the borrower's credit score, and possibly even legal action from the lender.

3. **Inability to Refinance or Modify the Loan :** If a borrower doesn't understand the terms and conditions of their loan, they may be unaware of their ability to refinance or modify the loan. **Consequently** this can restrict their options when facing financial difficulties or realizing that their existing loan terms no longer align with their requirements.

4. **Negative Impact on Credit Score :** Failure to understand the terms and conditions of a loan can also have a negative impact on a borrower's credit score. Late payments or defaulting on a loan can result in a decline in the credit score, making it more difficult to obtain credit in the future.

Steps to Ensure Understanding of Loan Terms and Conditions

1. **Read the Loan Agreement Carefully :** The first step to understanding the terms and a condition of a loan is to **thoroughly** read the loan agreement. It is **vital to allocate sufficient** time to review all of the terms, conditions, and fees associated with the loan. **Moreover,** borrowers should not hesitate to ask questions if there is any **aspect** they **find unclear or do not fully comprehend.**

2. **Seek Professional Advice :** If a borrower **feels uncertain** about the terms and conditions of a loan, they can seek professional advice. Financial advisors, loan officers, and attorneys can all provide guidance and assist borrowers in gaining a better understanding of the loan agreement. **Rupyaapaisa.com** also plays a vital role in guiding and mentoring individuals at the time of planning any loans.

3. **Use Online Resources :** Many online resources are available to help borrowers better understand loan terms and conditions. Borrowers can use online calculators to estimate the total cost of the loan, compare different loan options, and research the reputation of potential lenders.

4. **Negotiate the Terms of the Loan :** Borrowers can also negotiate the terms of the loan with the lender. This may **involve** negotiating a lower interest rate, **requesting the** waiver of certain fees, or extending the

loan term. **Through these negotiations,** borrowers can align the loan terms with their financial situation and **requirements more effectively.**

Few examples of Confusing Loan Terms

Loan agreements can contain **numerous complex** terms and conditions that may be difficult for borrowers to understand. Some common examples include:

1. **APR (Annual Percentage Rate) :** This **represents the interest** rate the borrower will pay on the loan, inclusive of any associated fees or charges.

2. **Amortization Schedule :** This schedule illustrates how the loan will be repaid over time, **specifying** payment amounts, interest rates, and the remaining principal balance.

3. **Balloon Payment :** This is a large payment that is due at the end of the loan term, which can be difficult for borrowers to afford.

4. **Collateral :** This is an asset that the borrower pledges as security for the loan, which the lender can seize if the borrower defaults on the loan.

5. **Prepayment Penalty :** This is a fee that the borrower may have to pay if they pay off the loan early.

Understanding these terms can empower borrowers to make informed decisions and navigate their loan agreements more effectively.

Tips for Reading and Understanding Loan Agreements

1. **Read the Agreement Thoroughly :** It's important to read the loan agreement thoroughly to ensure that you understand all of the terms and conditions. Don't be afraid to ask questions if there is something you don't understand.

2. **Highlight Key Terms :** Use a highlighter to mark essential terms and conditions in the loan agreement, such as the interest rate, payment schedule, and any fees or charges.

3. **Check the Fine Print :** Be **diligent in** checking the fine print for any hidden fees or charges that may not be immediately apparent.

4. **Ask for Clarification :** If **there is uncertainty** about any of the terms or conditions of the loan agreement, don't hesitate to ask the lender for clarification.

Consequences of Not Understanding Loan Terms

1. **Unexpected Fees and Charges : Failing to** understand loan terms can result in unexpected fees and charges that can make it difficult to repay the loan.

2. **Defaulting on the Loan :** If a borrower lacks understanding of the loan's terms and conditions, they may face the risk of defaulting on the loan, which can entail severe consequences.

3. **Inability to Refinance or Modify the Loan :** If a borrower doesn't understand the terms and conditions of the loan, they may not be aware of their options for refinancing or modifying the loan if their financial situation changes.

4. **Damage to Credit Score :** Late payments or defaulting on a loan can lead to decline in credit score, rendering it more challenging to obtain credit in the future.

Conclusion

Not understanding the terms and conditions of a loan can **carry significance** for borrowers, including unexpected fees, defaulting on the loan and damage to their credit score. By dedicating time to **thoroughly** reading the loan agreement, highlighting essential terms, checking the fine print, and seeking clarification when necessary, borrowers can ensure that they fully understand the terms and conditions of the loan and make well-informed financial decisions.

> "Money doesn't grow on trees, but it multiplies when you invest it wisely."
>
> ~Idowu Koyenikan

Chapter 3

Borrowing More Than You Need

Borrowing money can be an **essential** step in achieving financial **objectives, such as buying** a home or starting a business. **Nevertheless** it's crucial to borrow only the **necessary amount and avoid the** pitfall of borrowing **beyond one's realistic repayment capacity.** In this chapter, we'll explore the risks and consequences of borrowing more than you need, as well as tips for determining the appropriate loan amount.

The Risks and Consequences of Borrowing More Than You Need

Borrowing more than **necessary** can have serious consequences **on** your financial well-being. Here are some of the risks:

1. **Higher Interest Rates : By borrowing more than required**, you end up paying interest on funds that you don't actually need. **Consequently,** you'll incur more

interest expenses over the loan's duration **compared to borrowing only the necessary amount.**

2. **Difficulty Repaying the Loan** : Borrowing more than you need can make it more difficult to repay the loan, especially if your income or financial situation changes. This can lead to missed payments, late fees, and even defaulting on the loan.

3. **Damage to Credit Score :** Late payments and defaulting on a loan can have a negative impact on your credit score, making it more difficult to obtain credit in the future.

4. **Long-Term Financial Consequences** : Borrowing more than you need can lead to long-term financial consequences, including accumulating excessive debt that becomes difficult to manage and **necessitating** sacrifices in other aspects of your life to repay the debt.

Tips for Determining the Appropriate Loan Amount

1. **Calculate Your Expenses** : Before taking out a loan, calculate your expenses and determine exactly how much money you need. This can include items such as rent/mortgage, utilities, groceries, and other necessities.

2. **Consider Future Needs:** While calculating expenses, also **contemplate** any future **requirements that** may arise. For example, if you're taking out a business loan,

consider how much money you'll need to expand the business in the future.

3. **Research Interest Rates: Conduct** research interest rates offered by multiple lenders to identify what is reasonable for the loan amount you need. This can help you avoid borrowing more than you need at a high interest rate.

4. **Consult with Financial Advisors:** If **uncertain** about the **appropriate borrowing amount**, consider seeking advice from a financial advisor or other qualified professional. They can determine the suitable loan amount based on your financial circumstances and objectives.

Strategies for Reducing the Loan Amount

If you determine that you need to borrow **lower amount than initially anticipated**, here are some strategies for reducing the loan amount:

1. **Cut Expenses:** Look for ways to trim expenses, such as reducing dining out or canceling subscriptions, to allocate more funds towards loan payments.

2. **Increase Income: Explore opportunities for additional income by taking on a part-time job or engaging in a side hustle. This can accelerate your loan repayment and help you borrow less overall.**

3. **Use Savings:** If you have savings, consider using some of it to cover expenses instead of borrowing the entire amount.

Conclusion

Overborrowing can put you in a difficult financial situation with long-term consequences. To avoid this, determine the appropriate loan amount by considering your expenses, future needs, and interest rates. If you realize borrowing less is necessary, employ strategies like cutting expenses, increasing income, or using savings. By adopting responsible borrowing practices, you can achieve your financial goals while safeguarding yourself from precarious financial situations.

> "Money is a terrible master but an excellent servant."
>
> ~P.T. Barnum

Chapter 4

Focusing only on the Monthly Payment

When it comes to taking out a loan, it's **crucial to look beyond** the monthly payment and overlook other important factors that can affect the overall cost of the loan. In this chapter, we'll explore the dangers of focusing only on the monthly payment, how monthly payments are calculated, the difference between a low monthly payment and a low overall cost, and the importance of considering interest rates and fees.

The Dangers of Focusing Only on the Monthly Payment

Focusing **solely** on the monthly payment can pose risks as it may lead to longer loan terms and increased overall costs. Lenders are aware that borrowers often prioritize a low monthly payment, and they may capitalize on this by offering extended loan terms or higher interest rates, which ultimately result in higher overall expenses.

By focusing solely on the monthly payment, borrowers may also overlook other important factors, such as fees, prepayment penalties, and variable interest rates. This oversight can lead to unexpected costs and financial difficulties in the future.

How Monthly Payments are Calculated

Monthly payments on loans are calculated using a variety of factors, including the principal amount borrowed, the interest rate, and the loan term. The principal amount denotes the sum of the amount borrowed, while the interest rate represents the percentage charged on as interest throughout the loan's duration. On the other hand, the loan term is the length of time over which the loan is repaid.

Using these factors, lenders use an amortization formula to determine the monthly payment. This formula **considers both** the interest and principal payments over the life of the loan, and divides them into equal monthly payments.

The Difference between a Low Monthly Payment and a Low Overall Cost

It's important to understand that a low monthly payment does not necessarily indicate a low overall cost. In reality, a low monthly payment may imply a longer loan term, **subsequently** increasing the total amount of interest paid over the life of the loan.

For example, let's say you're considering two business loans of 10 lakh each. Loan A has a monthly payment of

Rs. 24318 and a loan term of 60 months, while Loan B has a monthly payment of Rs. 35160 and a loan term of 36 months. **Although Loan A boasts** a lower monthly payment, it **also carries** a longer loan term, **resulting in an additional interest cost of Rs. 193430 compared to Loan B.This example demonstrates that focusing solely on the monthly payment can lead to higher overall costs in the form of increased interest payments. It is vital to consider the loan term and the associated interest rates when evaluating the true cost of borrowing.**

The Importance of Considering Interest Rates and Fees

When borrowing money, it's important to consider not only the monthly payment but also the interest rate and any fees associated with the loan. Interest rates can vary widely depending on the type of loan and the lender, and even a small difference in interest rates can have a significant impact on the overall cost of the loan.

Fees can also add up quickly, so it's important to understand what fees are associated with the loan and how they will affect the overall cost. Some common fees include application fees, origination fees, and prepayment penalties.

Additionally, **it is worth noting that certain** loans may feature variable interest rates, which mean the interest rate can fluctuate over time. This **variability** can make it difficult to predict future payments and could lead to higher costs over the life of the loan.

Strategies for Avoiding Focusing Only on the Monthly Payment

To avoid the dangers of focusing solely on the monthly payment, it's important to take a holistic approach when considering a loan. This includes considering the interest rate, fees, loan term, and overall cost of the loan.

To determine the appropriate loan amount and monthly payment, consider your budget and financial goals. Determine how much you can comfortably afford to borrow and repay, and choose a loan with a monthly payment that fits within your budget.

Additionally, consider prepayment options and fees. If you have plans to pay off the loan **before its scheduled term, it is advisable to** look for loans that do not impose any prepayment penalties. This can help you save money on interest and effectively reduce **the overall cost of the loan.**

> "Money is a tool, not a goal. Money has no
> value until you exchange
> it for something you really need or want."
>
> ~Tony Robbins

Chapter 5

Ignoring Your Credit Score

When it comes to borrowing money, your credit score is one of the most important factors that lenders consider. **However,** many people make the mistake of ignoring their credit score or not understanding how it impacts their ability to obtain a loan and the terms they are offered.

In this chapter, we will explain what a credit score is, how it affects your ability to borrow money, and what you can do to improve your score.

What is a Credit Score?

A credit score is a three-digit number that is calculated based on your credit history. It **encompasses various** factors, such as your payment history, the amount of debt you have, credit history duration, and the types of credit you have utilized.

Why is Your Credit Score Important?

Your credit score is important because it is one of the key factors that lenders consider when deciding whether to approve your loan application. A high credit score indicates that you are a responsible borrower who is likely to repay your debts on time and in full. **Consequently,** this can lead to lower interest rates, more favorable loan terms, and the potential for higher loan amounts.

On the other hand, a low credit score can make it **challenging** to get approved for a loan, or it may result in higher interest rates and less favorable loan terms. In certain instances, you may even face credit denial altogether.

How to Check Your Credit Score

You can check your credit score for free from each of the three major credit bureaus (Equifax, Experian, and TransUnion) once per year. **Additionally,** you can utilize free credit score monitoring services to continuously keep track of your score.

If you discover that your credit score is lower than you anticipated, it is crucial to determine the reason behind it. Review your credit report for any inaccuracies, such as accounts that do not belong to you or incorrect reporting of late payments. **If you identify any errors, make sure to** dispute them with the credit bureau **responsible for** reporting them.

How to Improve Your Credit Score

Improving your credit score takes time and effort, but it's worth it in the long run. Here are some steps you can take to **enhance** your credit score:

1. **Pay your bills on time:** Late payments can have a significant impact on your credit score. Set up automatic payments or reminders to ensure you never miss a payment.

2. **Keep your credit utilization low:** Your credit utilization refers to the amount of credit you use compared to your credit limit. Aim to keep it below 30% to demonstrate responsible credit management to lenders.

3. **Avoid opening too many new accounts at once:** Each time you apply for credit, it results in a hard inquiry on your credit report, which can lower your score. Avoid opening multiple new accounts in a short period of time.

4. **Keep old credit accounts open:** The length of your credit history is an important factor in your score. Keeping old accounts open showcases to lenders that you have a long history of responsible credit management.

5. **Monitor your credit report regularly:** Check your credit report for errors and dispute any inaccuracies with the credit bureau responsible for reporting them.

Remember, improving your credit score is a gradual process, so be patient and consistent with your efforts.

The Consequences of Applying for Loans with a Low Credit Score

Applying for loans with a low credit score can result in several consequences, such as:

1. **Loan Denial:** Many lenders have a minimum credit score requirements, and if your score falls below that threshold, your loan application may be denied.

2. **Higher Interest Rates:** If you are approved for a loan with a low credit score, the interest rate offered to may be significantly higher compared to someone with a good credit score. Consequently, you'll end up paying more interest over the life of the loan.

3. **Higher Monthly Payments:** Higher interest rates also result in higher monthly payments. This can strain your budget and leave you with less money for other expenses.

4. **Longer Repayment Period:** If you're offered a high-interest loan, you may end up with a longer repayment period. This means you'll be paying off the loan for a more extended period, which can be financially burdensome.

In conclusion, ignoring your credit score can prove to be a costly mistake when seeking to borrow money. By understanding what a credit score is, how it impacts your ability to borrow money, and how to improve it, you can enhance your chances of getting approved for a loan with favorable terms.

> "If you want to be rich, think of ways to create value, not ways to make money."
>
> ~Naval Ravikant

Chapter **6**

The Importance of Shopping Around for Loans

Taking out a loan is a **significant** financial decision, and it's important to exercise due diligence when selecting a lender. One of the most common mistakes individuals make when taking out a loan is not **engaging in thorough research to find** the best deal. This **oversight** can lead to paying excessive amounts in interest and fees, **as well as agreeing to** loan terms that don't align with your needs.

Explanation of Not Shopping Around

When you fail to shop around for a loan, you **run the risk of overlooking** better interest rates and terms that could **result in long-term** savings. Each lender has their own interest rates, fees, and repayment terms, making it vital to compare multiple options before making a decision.

For example, if you're looking for a personal loan to consolidate debt, you may discover that one lender offers a lower interest compared to another. By neglecting to shop around, you could end up paying hundreds or even thousands of dollars in additional interest charges throughout the duration of the loan.

Tips for Shopping Around

To find the most suitable loan for your needs, start by conducting thorough research. Examine various lenders and loan options, and carefully compare the interest rates, fees, repayment terms, and other relevant factors that hold significance to you.

Additionally, It's also important to read the fine print and understand the terms and conditions of the loan before accepting it. Don't hesitate to ask questions and clarify any confusing terms or conditions.

Furthermore, consider the option of working with a financial advisor or credit counselor who can help you navigate the lending process and offer advice on the most advantageous loan options tailored to your specific situation.

The Consequences of Not Shopping Around

Not shopping around for a loan can result in paying more in interest and fees than necessary. It can also lead to accepting unfavorable loan terms or agreeing to a loan that doesn't meet your needs.

Additionally, applying for multiple loans without shopping around can have a negative impact on your credit score. Each loan application results in a hard inquiry on your credit report, which can lower your score and make it more difficult to get approved for future loans or credit.

In conclusion, taking the time to shop around and compare loan options is crucial for securing the best deal possible and avoiding unnecessary costs and fees. Be sure to conduct thorough your research, consider all factors, and understand the terms and conditions of any loan you're considering. Remember, the additional effort you invest in shopping around can yield significant long-term savings.

> "You must gain control over your money or the lack of it will forever control you."
>
> ~Dave Ramsey

Chapter 7

The Importance of Using a Loan for the Right Purpose

When taking out a loan, it's important to use the funds for their intended purpose. Although it may be tempting to allocate the loan towards other expenses, doing so can result in serious consequences. In this chapter, we'll discuss the risks associated with using a loan for the wrong purpose and underscore the significance of adhering to your financial goals.

The Dangers of Using a Loan for the Wrong Purpose

Using a loan for the wrong purpose can lead to a number of negative consequences. First and foremost, it can result in excessive debt that becomes challenging to repay. For instance, if you opt for a personal loan to buy a new car instead of using an auto loan, you may end up paying a much higher interest rate compared to what you would have obtained with an auto loan.

Additionally, utilizing a loan for the wrong purpose can lead to financial instability and missed payments. Suppose you use a business loan to cover personal expenses. In that case, you may encounter **difficulties in meeting loan** payments when unexpected business expenses arise.

Tips for Using a Loan for the Right Purpose

When taking out a loan, it's important to have a clear plan for how you will use the funds. Consider creating a budget or financial plan to help you stay on track with your goals and avoid overspending.

Furthermore, it is crucial to thoroughly read the loan agreement carefully and understand any restrictions or requirements on how the funds can be used. If you have any questions or concerns, don't hesitate to reach out to your lender for clarification.

The Importance of Staying on Track

Staying on track with your financial goals is crucial for long-term financial stability. Using a loan for the wrong purpose can hinder your progress and make it more difficult to achieve your goals.

Instead, prioritize using loans for their intended purpose and adhere to your budget and financial plan. This approach will assist you in avoiding unnecessary debt and accomplishing your goals more efficiently and swiftly.

In conclusion, using a loan for the wrong purpose can have serious consequences, including excessive debt and financial instability. To avoid these risks, ensure that you use loans for their intended purpose, carefully review loan agreements, and remain dedicated to your financial goals. By doing so, you can achieve long-term financial stability and achieve success.

> "Wealth is not about having a lot of money; it's about having a lot of options."
>
> ~Chris Rock

Chapter **8**

Not having a Plan for Repayment

Taking out a loan can **serve as an effective method to** finance substantial purchases or unexpected expenses, but it's important to have a solid plan for repayment. Failing to do so can lead to serious financial consequences, including damaged credit and even bankruptcy. In this chapter, we'll discuss the importance of having a repayment plan and strategies for creating one.

The Importance of a Repayment Plan

When you take out a loan, you are **effectively** entering into a contractual agreement with a lender. This contract includes various terms and conditions related to repayment, including the loan duration, interest rates, and payment schedules. It's important to carefully review these terms and create a plan for repayment that aligns with your budget and financial goals.

One of the **most significant errors individuals commit** when taking out a loan is assuming that they'll be able to make payments without a concrete plan. **Unfortunately,** unexpected expenses or fluctuations in income can swiftly disrupt even the most well-intentioned repayment plans. Without a clear strategy, it's easy to fall behind on payments and accumulate debt, leading to financial stress and potential default on the loan.

Creating a Repayment Plan

Creating a repayment plan involves three key steps: understanding the loan terms, evaluating your budget, and making a payment schedule.

1. **Understanding the Loan Terms: Begin by carefully examining** the loan terms and understand the details of the loan, such as the interest rate, payment schedule, and any associated fees or penalties for early or late payments. Make sure you fully understand the terms and conditions before creating a repayment plan.

2. **Evaluating Your Budget:** Next, evaluate your budget to determine how much you can realistically afford to pay each month. Consider your income, expenses, and existing debts. It is essential to be honest with yourself about your ability to make payments, and be sure to leave some wiggle room in case of unexpected expenses.

3. **Making a Payment Schedule:** Once you have a clear understanding of the loan terms and your budget, it's time to create a payment schedule. This should include the amount of each payment, the due dates, and the preferred method of payment. To avoid missing **any payments and incurring late fees,** consider setting up automatic payments.

Strategies for Repayment

In addition to creating a repayment plan, there are several strategies that can aid in paying off your loan more quickly and efficiently.

1. **Make Extra Payments:** If you have **surplus funds available,** consider allocating them towards your loan. Making extra payments can expedite the loan pay off process and reduce the overall interest you'll pay.

2. **Refinance or Consolidate:** If you have multiple loans or high-interest debt, consider refinancing or consolidating your loans. This can potentially lower your interest rate and simplify your repayment process.

3. **Prioritize High-Interest Loans:** If you have multiple loans, prioritize repayment of loans with the highest interest rates. This approach will save you money in the long run and **facilitate a faster journey towards becoming debt-free.**

Conclusion

Taking out a loan can be a helpful financial tool, but it's important to have a plan for repayment. Failing to do so can lead to serious financial consequences, including damaged credit and default on the loan. By understanding the loan terms, evaluating your budget, and creating a payment schedule, you can develop a clear plan for repayment and progress towards becoming debt-free.

> "Rule No. 1: Never lose money.
> Rule No. 2: Never forget Rule No.1."
>
> ~Warren Buffett

Conclusion: Recap of common mistakes and strategies for avoiding them

Taking out a loan can **initially seem overwhelming,** but with the right information and approach, it can also be a beneficial tool for achieving your financial goals. Throughout this guide, we have highlighted several common mistakes that borrowers often make when taking out loans and provided strategies for avoiding them. Here, we will recap these mistakes and summarize the key takeaways.

One common mistake is not understanding the terms and conditions of the loan. This can lead to confusion and even financial consequences down the road. To avoid this, borrowers should carefully read and ask questions about the loan agreement, paying close attention to factors such as interest rates, fees, and any penalties associated with early repayment.

Another mistake is borrowing more funds than necessary. This can lead to excessive debt and difficulties in repayment. To avoid this, borrowers should carefully assess their financial needs and only take out the amount they require. They should also explore alternative funding sources, such as grants or crowd funding, before resorting to loans is also recommended.

Focusing solely on the monthly payment is another mistake that borrowers frequently make. While a lower monthly payment may initially appear appealing, it can ultimately result in a higher overall cost due to extended repayment terms and higher interest rates. To avoid this, borrowers should look at the total cost of the loan, including interest rates and fees, and choose the option that offers the lowest overall cost.

Ignoring one's credit score is another common mistake. A low credit score can lead to higher interest rates and even rejection of loan applications. To avoid this, borrowers should check their credit score regularly and take proactive steps to improve it before applying for loans. These steps may include paying off outstanding debts, **rectifying any inaccuracies** on credit reports, and making timely payments on bills and loans.

Not shopping around for the best loan is yet another mistake that borrowers make. By not comparing loan options, borrowers may overlook better interest rates, fees, and repayment terms. To avoid this error, borrowers should conduct thorough research and compare multiple loan options before choosing the one that suits their needs and aligns with their budget.

Lastly, not having a plan for repayment can be a major mistake. Without a clear plan **outlining how the loan will be repaid,** borrowers may struggle to make timely payments or even default on the loan. To avoid this, borrowers should create a repayment plan that includes a budget, a defined timeline, and a contingency strategy for unexpected expenses or changes in income.

In conclusion, taking out a loan requires careful consideration and planning in order to avoid common mistakes. By thoroughly understanding the terms and conditions of the loan, borrowing only what is necessary, considering the overall cost of the loan, taking steps to improve credit scores, shopping around for the best loan, and having a repayment plan, borrowers can make the most of their loan and achieve their financial goals.

> "It's not how much money you make, but how much money you keep, how hard it works for you, and how many generations you keep it for."
>
> ~Robert Kiyosaki

Hire an expert who can help in planning your loan

When it comes to borrowing money, **being** well-informed and making smart decisions is crucial. With so many different types of loans available and a wide range of lenders to choose from, it can be difficult to know where to start. This is where hiring an expert like rupyaapaisa.com can be extremely helpful.

Rupyaapaisa.com is an online platform that connects borrowers with a network of trusted and reliable lenders. They offer an extensive range of loan products, including personal loans, home loans, business loans, and more. One of the biggest benefits of working with rupyaapaisa.com is **their** team of financial experts who can help you plan your loan and make well-informed decisions.

Here are some of the ways in which rupyaapaisa.com can help you with your loan planning:

1. **Assessing Your Financial Needs:** One of the initial steps in planning your loan is to determine how much money you need to borrow. The financial experts at rupyaapaisa.com can help you assess your financial needs and determine the appropriate loan amount based on your income, expenses, and other financial obligations.

2. **Choosing the Right Loan Product: With numerous loan options** available, each with its own set of features

and benefits. The financial experts at rupyaapaisa.com can guide you to understand the differences between various loan products and assist you in selecting the one that aligns best with your needs.

3. **Comparing Lenders:** Once you have chosen the suitable loan product, it is important to compare lenders to secure the best possible deal. The financial experts at rupyaapaisa.com can help you compare interest rates, fees, and other terms and conditions **across various lenders. This ensures that you can identify the lender offering the most favorable overall value.**

4. **Understanding Loan Terms and Conditions:** Loan agreements can be complex and difficult to understand. The financial experts at rupyaapaisa.com can help you read and understand the terms and conditions of your loan agreement, ensuring that you are fully informed and aware of your obligations.

5. **Creating a Repayment Plan:** Finally, it is important to have a plan in place for repaying your loan. The financial experts at rupyaapaisa.com can help you create a **customized** repayment plan that fits your budget and ensures that you are able to pay off your loan in a timely manner.

In conclusion, **the process of** borrowing money can be a complicated process, and it is important to have the right support and guidance. By hiring an expert like rupyaapaisa.com, you can **effectively** plan your loan, make well-informed decisions, that will help you achieve your financial goals.

> "When money realizes that it is in good hands, it wants to stay and multiply in those hands."
>
> ~Idowu Koyenikan

About the Author

In the world of Small and Medium-sized Enterprises (SMEs), few names shine as brightly as Mr. Mukesh Pandey. For more than 18 years of his life, he has been devoted to helping SMEs, doctors, and chartered accountants get a solid start and succeed in the challenging business landscape. Being recognized and awarded as the best SME consultant is proof of his valuable contributions in the MSME (Micro, Small, and Medium Enterprises) and professional sectors.

The Early Years

Mukesh Pandey's early life tells a story of determination and ambition. He came to Delhi with very few resources but a strong drive to succeed. His career began as a sales executive at American Express Bank, a crucial turning point that gave him valuable knowledge and skills in the financial services industry. His dedication and passion for his work did not go unnoticed. He quickly climbed the ranks, eventually reaching the position of an area sales manager at

Yes Bank. In this role, he supervised a team of 15 members in the LAP (Loan Against Property) and business loan areas, showcasing his hard work and excellence in the competitive world of finance.

SME Consultant: A Vision to Help MSMEs Soar

In 2009, Mukesh Pandey made a big decision. He left his job in a big company to start his own consulting firm. His goal was to help small and medium-sized businesses, called SMEs, do better. He wanted them to grow and succeed. This is important because SMEs create jobs and help the economy, so it's a good thing he's doing.

Mr. Pandey is really good at raising money. He knows how to make smart plans to get money for SMEs, doctors, and chartered accountants who want to grow. He comes up with new and creative ways to raise money, making it easier for businesses to grow. This helps SMEs succeed, and it shows that Mr. Mukesh Pandey is a trusted advisor in SME consulting.

Testimonials of Success

When happy clients share their thoughts, it's like a strong vote of confidence in Mukesh Pandey's work. These words don't just show how good he is, but also the real and good things he's done for the people he's helped. These stories might make other people want his help in their businesses too.'

Contributions as an Author and Thought Leader

Mukesh Pandey doesn't just help businesses with advice; he is also an accomplished author and a person with smart ideas. His books, "Take Control and Master Your Loan" and "Unleash Your Business Potential," reflect his commitment to sharing his wealth of knowledge with the business community. These books offer invaluable insights and practical guidance for SMEs, entrepreneurs, and business owners, providing them with the tools to navigate the complexities of finance, loans, and business growth. By writing these influential books, Mr. Pandey has established himself as an authority in the field. Now he's a great resource for individuals and businesses who want to do well in the challenging world of SMEs.

Media Maven: The Voice of Authority

Mukesh Pandey is an important person in SMEs and business growth. He writes articles in famous newspapers like the Times of India. These articles help many people by giving them good advice and smart ideas. This helps lots of small businesses do well. Mukesh is like a media expert, and his dedication to helping small and medium-sized businesses is really admirable.

A Trusted Voice in the Media

Mukesh Pandey is a well-respected and trusted expert in the field of small businesses and their growth. He's so good at what he does that he's often asked to share his knowledge on TV and in discussions. He's been on famous news channels like Aaj Tak, CNBC Awaaz, India TV, and News 24. Many people watch and listen to him to learn from his smart ideas. Mukesh is like the person you can trust for good advice in the world of business and small enterprises.

Conclusion

Mukesh Pandey's journey as an SME consultant is remarkable. His story, from humble beginnings to becoming a trusted and recognized authority in the world of Small and Medium-sized Enterprises, is inspiring. His dedication, financial expertise, and commitment to the growth of SMEs have left an indelible mark on the MSME community. Through his books, articles, and media appearances, Mukesh Pandey has shared invaluable insights, empowering entrepreneurs and business owners nationwide. He is not just a consultant but also a guiding light for those who aspire to unlock their business potential and take control of their financial future. Mukesh has done a lot for the business world, and his story inspires many in the SME community.